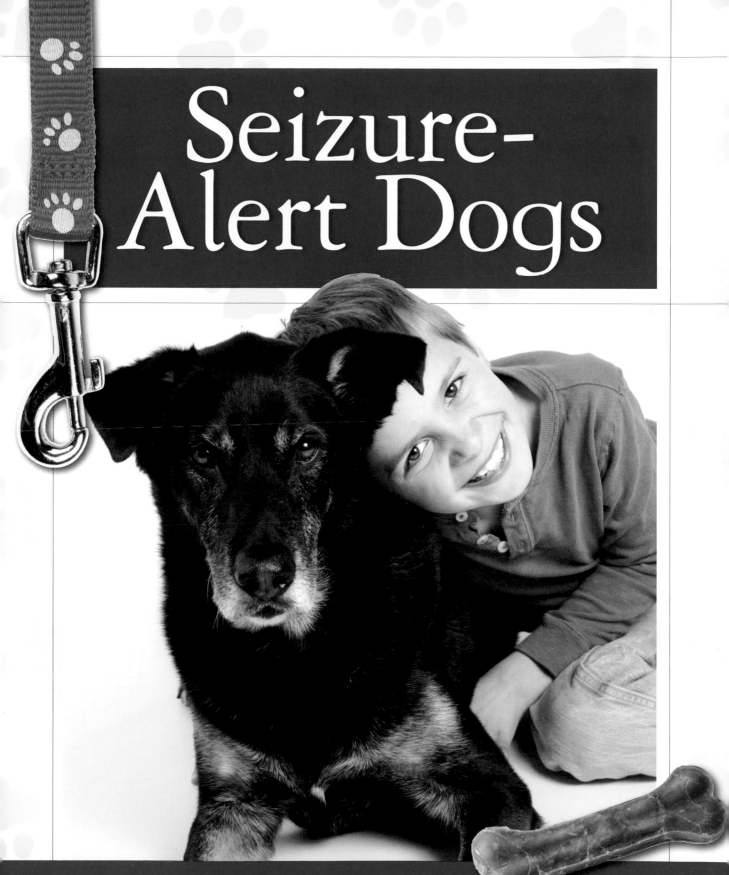

Seizure-Alert Dogs

BY KARA L. LAUGHLIN

Published by The Child's World®
1980 Lookout Drive • Mankato, MN 56003-1705
800-599-READ • www.childsworld.com

ACKNOWLEDGMENTS
The Child's World®: Mary Berendes, Publishing Director
The Design Lab: Design
Jody Jensen Shaffer: Editing
Pamela J. Mitsakos: Photo Research

PHOTO CREDITS
© Andrew Burgess: leash; Anna Hoychuk/Shutterstock.com:
cover, 1; AP Photo/The Gleaner, Mike Lawrence: 4; AP Photo/
The Post-Register, Chris Hatch: 7; HongChan00Dreamstime.
com: 14; Jaromir Chalabala/Shutterstock.com: 9; Jovanka_
Novakovic/iStock.com: 16; Lee319/Shutterstock.com: 21;
Michelle D. Milliman/Shutterstock.com: 19; remik44992: bone;
Tina Rencelj/Shutterstock.com: 11; Yifoto/Dreamstime.com12-13

ISBN 9781626873124
LCCN 2014934412

Printed in the United States of America
Mankato, MN
July, 2014
PA02219

ABOUT THE AUTHOR

Kara L. Laughlin is the author of eleven books for kids. She lives in Virginia with her husband and three children. They don't have a dog…yet!

TABLE OF CONTENTS

Fortune-Telling Dogs?

Can dogs predict the future? Some people with **seizures** think so. Seizures are like lightning storms that happen in the brain. When they happen, people can't control their bodies. They might jerk their arms and legs. They might fall down. They might seem to be asleep. Seizures can last a few seconds or a few minutes. They are sort of like the hiccups: they start all of a sudden. People can't stop them. They don't know when they will end. But seizures are much more scary than hiccups.

For a long time, people said that their dogs knew when their seizures were coming. In the 1990s some doctors tried to find out if that was true. They asked people with **seizure disorders** about their dogs. Some dogs did seem to know when seizures were on the way. Then doctors had a new question. How?

Alex's dog Lady alerts him to when he is about to have a seizure.

Still a Mystery

How do dogs predict seizures? Scientists don't know for sure. What they think is that dogs can smell seizures. Our bodies make smells all the time. People might smell a tiny bit different before a seizure. We wouldn't notice such a small change, but dogs might. They might learn that the new smell means a seizure is on the way.

No matter how they do it, the dogs don't really tell the future. Seizures have three parts: the beginning, the middle, and the end. The beginning is called the **aura**. Many people who have seizures don't notice the aura. When dogs notice a seizure, they are noticing the aura, or first part, of a seizure.

INTERESTING FACT
Sometimes seizures end during the aura. A dog who alerts early might seem to be wrong if the seizure ends.

Cade's dog Baxter helps Cade know when a seizure is about to start.

Seizure-Response Dogs

There are two kinds of seizure dogs. **Seizure-response dogs** help during a seizure. **Seizure-alert dogs** warn when one is coming.

Seizure-response dogs learn to do whatever their owners need them to do. Some get help. Some stay with their owner. Some get medicine. Some pull their owners to a safe place. When the seizure is done, dogs might help their owners get up. They might just stay with them until they feel better.

INTERESTING FACT
Some people with seizure dogs program a button on their phones to call 911. If they have a seizure, their dogs are trained to bite the button to call for help.

Seizures can even happen when a person is sleeping. Many people sleep with their dogs. That way, if a seizure happens at night, the dog can help them.

A seizure-response dog is always aware, even at night.

Seizure-Alert Dogs

Seizure-alert dogs are special seizure-response dogs. They can warn their owners when a seizure is on the way. Some dogs learn to do this on their own. Some are trained to do it. There are lots of ways a dog might warn her owner. She might pace. She might lick her owner's hand. A dog might even nip at her owner.

A dog always gives the same amount of time to get ready. The amount of time is different for each dog though. Some dogs know a few hours before the seizure. Others only know a few minutes ahead. People and their dogs get to know each other well. People learn how much time they have to get ready.

A seizure-alert dog might lick its owner's hand to signal that a seizure is about to start.

Trouble with Training

Seizure dogs are trained like other service dogs. They learn how to behave in places where most dogs can't go. Usually, dog training goes like this: trainers get a dog to do what they want. Then they reward the dog. The dog learns that when he does the right thing, he will get a treat.

Training a seizure-alert dog is not like teaching a dog a simple trick.

Training a seizure-alert dog is more tricky. How do you know when to reward the dog? A dog might seem to warn about a seizure, but then it doesn't come. It won't work to reward a dog when there's no seizure coming. Some dogs warn of seizures hours ahead of time. If they don't get a treat until the seizure, it's too late! They don't know why they're getting the treat.

This is what trainers do. At first the dogs get a treat after every seizure. The dogs learn that something good comes after a seizure. In time, when the dog can tell a seizure is coming, she will do a special thing to ask for a seizure treat. Then the owner knows a seizure is coming.

Labradors like this one make great seizure-alert dogs.

What Makes a Good Seizure Dog?

Seizure dogs need to be good at a lot of things. They need to notice small things about the people they live with. They need to care about how people feel. They need to stay calm when their owners have seizures. They also need to like people. They need to be able to be good in public. That's a lot to need from a dog! Some breeds that make good seizure dogs are golden retrievers, Labrador retrievers, Irish setters, Samoyeds, border collies, and German shepherds.

INTERESTING FACT
Not many kinds of service dogs are given to children. But seizure dogs are. Some even go to school with their owners.

What Do Seizure Dogs Do All Day?

The vest a seizure dog wears is called a harness.

Seizure dogs are service dogs. They get to go where their owners go. They wear a vest called a **harness**. It lets people know that they are working dogs. Sometimes people with seizures don't want to leave the house. They worry that they'll have seizures while they're out. Seizure dogs help their owners to feel more calm about going out. Their owners know that if they have seizures, their dogs will take care of them.

Most of the time seizure dogs act like any pet. They play with their owners. They go for walks. If a seizure happens, they do what they are trained to do. The rest of the time, they stay close and ready to help.

If You Meet a Seizure Dog

When seizure dogs are at work, they need to focus on work. If you see a seizure dog, ask the owner before you pet it. Be ready for the owner to say, "No." The owner knows her dog best. She knows if petting will keep her dog from doing his job.

If you meet someone with a seizure dog, you might have lots of questions. Kids with seizure disorders want to just be kids. Asking lots of questions might make them uncomfortable. Try to save most of your questions until you are friends. If you have a lot of questions, you might want to read books or ask an adult to get answers.

Be sure to ask the owner before you approach a seizure-alert dog.

Evan Moss and Mindy

When Evan Moss was seven, he liked Pokemon and Phineas and Ferb. He also got three or four seizures a month. Evan wanted a seizure-alert dog. He found a place that would give him one. But first he had to raise some money. His family had to pay $13,000 for his dog!

Evan wrote a book about wanting a seizure dog. Part of it said, "The dog will eat pizza with me. If I go to the moon, it will go there with me." Evan sold his book on the Internet. He sold enough books to get Mindy, his seizure dog. He even had money left over. He used it to help seven other people get dogs.

INTERESTING FACT

Mindy goes everywhere with Evan. If Evan has to stay in the hospital, Mindy goes with him. Evan says, "The best thing about having Mindy is playing with her...I love racing with her."

Mindy is a goldendoodle (part golden retriever, part poodle). When Evan has a seizure coming, Mindy licks Evan in a special way. Then he knows to get ready for a seizure. Mindy barks if Evan has a seizure. Then Evan's parents take care of him. They give him medicine to stop his seizures.

Goldendoodles make great seizure-alert dogs. They are very smart and affectionate.

GLOSSARY

aura (OR-uh) An aura is the first part of a seizure. People don't always notice it, but many dogs do.

harness (HAR-ness) The vest a seizure-alert dog wears is called a harness.

seizure (SEE-zhur) A seizure is a time when people can't control their bodies. Seizures happen when too many brain cells turn on at once.

seizure-alert dogs (SEE-zhur uh-LERT DOGZ) Seizure-alert dogs are trained to let their owners know of a coming seizure.

seizure disorders (SEE-zhur diss-OR-durz) Seizure disorders are illnesses that can cause seizures.

seizure-response dogs (SEE-zhur ree-SPONS DOGZ) Seizure-response dogs are trained to act when a seizure occurs.

LEARN MORE

IN THE LIBRARY

Felty, Margaret. *Seizure-Alert Dogs.* New
York: Bearport Publishing. 2009.

Moss, Evan. *My Seizure Dog.* Amazon Digital Services. 2011.

ON THE WEB

Visit our Web site for links about seizure-alert dogs:
www.childsworld.com/links

*Note to Parents, Teachers, and Librarians: We routinely check our Web links to
make sure they're safe, active sites—so encourage your readers to check them out!*

INDEX